Birds of the Southwest

Adventure Quick Guides

YOUR WAY TO EASILY IDENTIFY BACKYARD BIRDS

Adventure Quick Guides

Organized by color for quick and easy identification, this guide covers 140 species of the most common birds found in Arizona, California, Colorado, Nevada, New Mexico, Texas and Utah.

KEY

- If the male and female of a species look the same or nearly the same, only one bird is shown.

- When the male and female are different colors, they are shown in their respective color sections with "male" or "female" labels.

Northern Cardinal
black mask, red bill
male red
female

- The smaller type indicates the color section in which the male/female counterpart is found.

- A feeder icon 🐦 indicates the bird visits backyard feeders.

SOUTHWEST BIRD FIELD GUIDES

For more information about nesting, young, migration and interesting gee-whiz facts, use Stan's field guides for these Southwest states: Arizona, California, Colorado, New Mexico, Texas and Utah.

STAN TEKIELA

Stan Tekiela is an award-winning photographer, naturalist and author of more than 175 field guides, nature books, children's books and other products about birds, mammals, reptiles, amphibians, trees, wildflowers and cacti.

Cover and book design by Lora Westberg
Edited by Sandy Livoti

15 14 13 12 11 10 9 8

Cover image by Stan Tekiela:
   Vermilion Flycatcher
All images copyrighted. Images by Stan Tekiela and contributing photographers: Maslowski Wildlife Productions and Brian E. Small.

Birds of the Southwest Quick Guide
Copyright © 2014 by Stan Tekiela
Published by Adventure Publications
An imprint of AdventureKEEN
310 Garfield Street South
Cambridge, Minnesota 55008
(800) 678-7006
www.adventurepublications.net
All rights reserved
Printed in China
ISBN 978-1-59193-410-3 (pbk.)

House Finch

brown cap

female brown

male

Purple Finch

red cap

female brown

male

Vermilion Flycatcher

crimson head, black eye line

male

female gray

Cassin's Finch

red head

female brown

male

Red Crossbill

long crossed bill

female yellow

male

Summer Tanager

overall red

female yellow

male

Northern Cardinal

black mask, red crest, red bill

female brown

male

5" 6" 6" 6 1/2" 6 1/2" 8" 8 1/2"

Allen's Hummingbird

reddish throat, female less orange

Rufous Hummingbird

burnt orange, red throat, female less orange

Orchard Oriole

black head, rusty body

female yellow

male

Bullock's Oriole

large white wing patch

female yellow

male

Hooded Oriole

black face, white wing bar

female yellow

male

Black-headed Grosbeak

black head, white wing bars

female brown

male

3 3/4"   3 3/4"   7 1/2"   8"   8"   8"

Mostly yellow

Lesser Goldfinch
female
male

black cap, female lacks black cap

Lawrence's Goldfinch
female
male

black face, female lacks black face

American Goldfinch
female
male

black forehead, female lacks black forehead

Orange-crowned Warbler

dull yellow, thin bill

Yellow Warbler

orange streaks on chest, female lacks streaks

Common Yellowthroat

black mask, female lacks mask

Dickcissel
female
male

black bib, female lacks bib

Red Crossbill

dull yellow, long crossed bill

male red

female

Western Tanager
female
male

yellow with red head, black wings, female olive wings

Orchard Oriole

dull yellow, white wing bars

male orange

female

4 1/2"   4 3/4"   5"   5"   5"   5"   6"   6 1/2"   7 1/4"   7 1/2"

Mostly yellow

Evening Grosbeak
female

bright yellow eyebrows, large ivory bill, female duller

male

Summer Tanager

large bill

male red

female

Bullock's Oriole

dirty yellow, white wing bars

male orange

female

Hooded Oriole

gray back, white wing bar

male orange

female

Scott's Oriole
female

black "hood," white wing bars, female less black

male

Western Kingbird

yellow belly, dark tail

Western Meadowlark

black V on chest, white outer tail feathers as seen in flight

8"   8"   8"   8"   9"   9"   9"

Calliope Hummingbird

rosy throat, female spotted throat

Costa's Hummingbird

tapering purple throat, female pale throat

Black-chinned Hummingbird

blue-to-black throat, female gray head

Anna's Hummingbird

rosy head and throat, female rosy flecks on throat

Broad-tailed Hummingbird

rosy throat, female spotted cheeks

Violet-green Swallow

green cap, white face, female duller

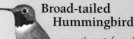

female

Painted Bunting

blue head, orange chest, female all green

male

Green-tailed Towhee

red cap, white throat

Lewis's Woodpecker

red face, gray collar

3 1/4" 3 1/2" 3 3/4" 4" 4" 5 1/4" 5 1/2" 7 1/4" 10 3/4"

Indigo Bunting

blue with dark wings

female brown

male

Lazuli Bunting

turquoise head, rusty chest

female brown

male

Tree Swallow

white chin and chest

Eastern Bluebird

sky blue with rusty chest, female duller

Mountain Bluebird

deep blue, female paler

Western Bluebird

rusty chest and flanks, female duller

Blue Grosbeak

rusty wing bars

female brown

male

Barn Swallow

orange forehead, forked tail, female duller

Purple Martin

female

nearly black, notched tail, female gray belly

male

Pinyon Jay

long straight bill, short tail

5 1/2"   5 1/2"   5 1/2"   7"   7"   7"   7"   7"   8 1/2"   11"

Mostly blue

Steller's Jay
black head, large crest

Woodhouse's Scrub-Jay
long tail, gray back

Mexican Jay
large black bill, gray chest

Belted Kingfisher
shaggy crest, female has two bands on chest

Mostly gray

Golden-crowned Kinglet
gold and orange on head, female lacks orange

Ruby-crowned Kinglet
white wing bars

Lucy's Warbler
orange crest and rump

Pygmy Nuthatch
gray cap

11"   11"   11 1/2"   13"   4"   4"   4"   4 1/4"

Mostly gray

Bushtit

tiny black bill

Red-breasted Nuthatch

black eye line, female gray cap

Verdin

yellow head, rusty shoulder patch, female duller

Black-capped Chickadee

black cap, white cheeks, white wing edges

Bridled Titmouse

bold head pattern, pointed crest, black chin

Mountain Chickadee

black line through eyes

Dark-eyed Junco

white belly, pink bill

male

female brown

White-breasted Nuthatch

black cap, white cheeks, female duller cap

Yellow-rumped Warbler

yellow patches, black chest, female streaked chest

Juniper Titmouse

small crest

4 1/2"   4 1/2"   4 1/2"   5"   5"   5 1/2"   5 1/2"   5 1/2"   5 1/2"   6"

Mostly gray

Black-throated Sparrow

black and white head, black throat

Vermilion Flycatcher

pinkish belly, dark tail

female

male red

Common Ground-Dove

gray nape, dark-tipped red bill

Say's Phoebe

peachy belly and undertail, black tail

Eastern Kingbird

white-tipped tail

Phainopepla

ragged crest, red eyes

male black

female

Townsend's Solitaire

white eye-ring

Gray Catbird

chestnut patch under tail

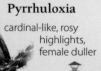

Pyrrhuloxia

cardinal-like, rosy highlights, female duller

Loggerhead Shrike

black mask

6"   6"   6 1/2"   7 1/2"   8"   8"   8 1/2"   9"   9"   9"

Mostly gray

Northern Mockingbird
long tail, white wing bars

American Robin
black head, female gray head

Gambel's Quail
rusty cap, black belly, female lacks bold markings

California Quail
brown cap, scaled belly, black chin, female lacks black chin

White-winged Dove
blue ring around eyes, white wing edges

Curve-billed Thrasher
large down-curved bill

Canada Jay
white forehead

Clark's Nutcracker
black wings and tail

Eurasian Collared-Dove
thin black line on neck

Rock Pigeon
variety of colors

10"   10"   10"   10"   11"   11"   11 1/2"   12"   12 1/2"   13"

Downy Woodpecker

short bill, red spot, female lacks red spot

Painted Redstart

red chest and belly

Lark Bunting

white wing bar

female brown

male

Black Phoebe

black head, white belly, pumps tail

Ladder-backed Woodpecker

black and white with red cap, female lacks red cap

Red-breasted Sapsucker

red head, chest and nape

Red-naped Sapsucker

red forehead and chin, female white chin

female

Williamson's Sapsucker

red chin, yellow belly, female brown head

male

Acorn Woodpecker

white eye-ring, red cap, female smaller red cap

Gila Woodpecker

brown head, red cap, female lacks red cap

6" 6" 6 1/2" 7" 7" 8 1/2" 8 1/2" 9" 9" 9"

Hairy Woodpecker

large bill, red spot, female lacks red spot

Golden-fronted Woodpecker

yellow nape, red cap, female lacks red cap

Scissor-tailed Flycatcher

pink wing linings, long tail, female shorter tail

Black-billed Magpie

black bill, long tail, female shorter tail

Mostly black

Brown-headed Cowbird

brown head, gray bill

male   female brown

European Starling

bill yellow in summer, gray in winter

Bronzed Cowbird

male   red eyes

female brown

Phainopepla

black ragged crest, red eyes

female gray

male

9"   9 1/2"   10"   20"   7 1/2"   7 1/2"   8"   8"

Spotted Towhee

white spots on back, red eyes

female brown

male

Red-winged Blackbird

red and yellow shoulder patches

female brown

male

Brewer's Blackbird

purplish head, yellow eyes

female brown

male

Yellow-headed Blackbird

yellow head, white wing patches

female brown

male

Common Grackle

blue head, long tail, female shorter tail

Great-tailed Grackle

purple head, long tail, yellow eyes

male

female brown

American Crow

black with familiar "caw" call

Chihuahuan Raven

hidden white neck feathers

Common Raven

shaggy throat feathers

8 1/2" 8 1/2" 9" 10" 12" 18" 18" 20" 24 1/2"

Mostly brown

Brown Creeper
long curved bill

House Finch
brown cap, streaked flanks and belly

male red

female

Pine Siskin
yellow streaks on wings, female less yellow

Chipping Sparrow
rusty cap, clear chest

Chimney Swift
pointed head and tail as seen in flight

House Wren
short curved bill

Indigo Bunting
brown with lighter throat

male blue

female

Lazuli Bunting
two narrow wing bars

male blue

female

Dark-eyed Junco
brown with white belly

male gray

female

Song Sparrow
central dark spot on streaked chest

5"   5"   5"   5"   5"   5"   5 1/2"   5 1/2"   5 1/2" 5 1/2"

Cliff Swallow

tan-to-rust forehead and cheeks

Bewick's Wren

white eyebrows, curved bill

Carolina Wren

white eyebrows, white markings on sides of neck

Canyon Wren
white throat, very long curved bill

Rock Wren

gray with fine speckles

Hermit Thrush

dark spots on chest, rusty tail

Gray-crowned Rosy-Finch

gray head, rosy sides, female less rosy

Purple Finch
white eye stripe

male red

female

American Tree Sparrow

rusty cap, central dark spot on clear chest

female

House Sparrow
black throat, gray cap, female tan eyebrows

male

5 1/2"   5 1/2"   5 1/2"   5 3/4"   6"   6"   6"   6"   6"   6"

Mostly brown

Lark Bunting

heavily streaked with two bold stripes on throat

male black & white

female

Cassin's Finch

heavily streaked chest and belly

male red

female

Lark Sparrow

bold head pattern, central dark spot on white chest

White-throated Sparrow

white chin, bold eyebrows

Fox Sparrow

heavily streaked chest and belly

White-crowned Sparrow

black and white head

Blue Grosbeak

brown with tan wing bars

male blue

female

Brown-headed Cowbird

whitish throat

male black

female

Horned Lark

white-to-yellow throat, black necklace, female duller

Cedar Waxwing

black mask, red wing tips

6 1/2" 6 1/2" 6 1/2" 6 1/2" 7" 7" 7" 7 1/2" 7 1/2" 7 1/2"

Bronzed Cowbird

red eyes

male black

female

Black-headed Grosbeak

white eyebrows

male orange

female

Spotted Towhee

brown head, red eyes

male black

female

Northern Cardinal

black mask, red bill

male red

female

Red-winged Blackbird

light eyebrows

male black

female

Cactus Wren

long white eyebrows, dark spots

Brewer's Blackbird

dark eyes, short dark bill

female

male black

Common Nighthawk

white chin, white band across wings as seen in flight, female tan chin

California Towhee

rusty undertail, faint streaks on chin

Canyon Towhee

rusty cap, dark necklace

8"   8"   8 1/2"   8 1/2"   8 1/2"   8 1/2"   9"   9"   9"   9"

Mostly brown

Abert's Towhee
dark face, pink bill

Yellow-headed Blackbird
dull yellow head and chest

female

male black

Gilded Flicker
brown cap, red mark on face, female lacks red mark

Killdeer
two black bands around neck

Northern Flicker
red wing linings, red mark on face, female lacks red mark

Mourning Dove
blue eye-ring, bobs head while walking

Great-tailed Grackle
long tail, white eyes

female

male black

Greater Roadrunner
large bill, long tail

female

Ring-necked Pheasant
long tail, white ring around neck, female all brown

female

male

Wild Turkey
bare skin on head, black beard, female lacks beard

male

9 1/2" 10"   11"   11"   12"   12"   18"   23"   33"   42"

Bird Feeding Guide

Bluebirds

Favorite: mealworms
Also: dried fruit

Cardinals

Favorite: black oil sunflower seeds
Also: striped sunflower seeds, safflower, millet, cracked corn,
peanut butter

Chickadees, Nuthatches & Titmice

Favorite: black oil sunflower seeds
Also: striped sunflower seeds, safflower, millet, Nyjer thistle,
peanut butter, suet, shelled peanuts, nectar, cracked
corn, mealworms, fruit

Doves

Favorite: millet
Also: cracked corn, safflower, hulled sunflower seeds, milo

Finches (including Grosbeaks & Crossbills)

Favorite: Nyjer thistle
Also: millet, black oil sunflower seeds, striped sunflower seeds,
hulled sunflower seeds, cracked corn, safflower, orange
halves, grape jelly

Hummingbirds

Favorite: nectar

Jays & Crows

Favorite: grape jelly
Also: shelled peanuts, black oil sunflower seeds, peanut butter,
whole or cracked corn, bread crumbs, dried fruit, suet, milo

Orioles

Favorite: grape jelly
Also: orange halves, mealworms, nectar

Sparrows (including Juncos & Towhees)

Favorite: cracked corn
Also: millet, black oil sunflower seeds, striped sunflower
seeds, hulled sunflower seeds, safflower

Woodpeckers (including Flickers & Sapsuckers)

Favorite: suet
Also: shelled peanuts, nuts, acorns, peanut butter, black oil
sunflower seeds, mealworms, dried fruit, orange halves,
whole corn, grape jelly

Adventure Quick Guides

Only Southwest Birds
Organized by color
for quick and easy identification

Simple and convenient—narrow your choices by color, and view just a few birds at a time

- Pocket-sized format—easier than laminated foldouts

- Professional photos showing key markings

- Bird feeder icon and feeding guide

- Silhouettes and sizes for quick comparison

- Based on Stan Tekiela's best-selling bird field guides

Improve your bird identification skills with these beautiful *Birds of the Southwest* Playing Cards

ISBN 978-1-59193-410-3 **$9.95**

5 0 9 9 5

Adventure PUBLICATIONS
an imprint of Adventure**KEEN**

NATURE/BIRDS/SOUTHWEST